SILLY SCHOOL RIDDLES

BY LISA EISENBERG

PICTURES BY ELWOOD H. SMITH

DIAL BOOKS FOR YOUNG READERS

DIAL BOOKS FOR YOUNG READERS
A division of Penguin Young Readers Group
Published by The Penguin Group
Penguin Group (USA) Inc., 375 Hudson Street, New York, NY 10014, U.S.A.
Penguin Group (Canada), 90 Eglinton Avenue East, Suite 700, Toronto, Ontario, Canada M4P
2Y3 (a division of Pearson Penguin Canada Inc.)
Penguin Books Ltd, 80 Strand, London WC2R 0RL, England
Penguin Ireland, 25 St. Stephen's Green, Dublin 2, Ireland (a division of Penguin Books Ltd)
Penguin Group (Australia), 250 Camberwell Road, Camberwell, Victoria 3124, Australia
(a division of Pearson Australia Group Pty Ltd)
Penguin Books India Pvt Ltd, 11 Community Centre,
Panchsheel Park, New Delhi - 110 017, India
Penguin Group (NZ), Cnr Airborne and Rosedale Roads, Albany, Auckland 1310,
New Zealand (a division of Pearson New Zealand Ltd)
Penguin Books (South Africa) (Pty) Ltd, 24 Sturdee Avenue,
Rosebank, Johannesburg 2196, South Africa
Penguin Books Ltd, Registered Offices: 80 Strand, London WC2R 0RL, England

The publisher does not have any control over and does not
assume any responsibility for author or third-party websites or their content.

Designed by Jasmin Rubero
Text set in Caslon 540
Manufactured in China on acid-free paper

The Dial Easy-to-Read logo is a registered trademark of Dial Books for Young Readers,
a division of Penguin Young Readers Group
® TM 1,162,718.

1 3 5 7 9 10 8 6 4 2

Library of Congress Cataloging-in-Publication Data
Eisenberg, Lisa.
Silly school riddles / by Lisa Eisenberg ; pictures by Elwood H. Smith.
p. cm.
ISBN 978-0-8037-3165-3
1. Schools—Juvenile humor. 2. Riddles, Juvenile. I. Smith, Elwood H., date. II. Title.
PN6231.S3E37 2008
398.6—dc22
2007022365

Reading Level 2.6

To Dylan, who already knows how to be silly
—Gran E.

With love to Gabe & Annie
—E.S.

Why should you be extra-careful during the back-to-school season?

Because it is the *fall* season!

Which state is the best place to buy school supplies?

Pencil-vania!

Why did the silly goose think
he had to walk to school?

He heard the first graders *took* the bus!

What kind of dance happens
every day at school?

Atten-dance!

What did one school locker say
to the other?

I'll *hallways* stand by you!

Did the silly goose learn how to tie his shoes the first day of kindergarten?

He did *knot*!

Which one of your school supplies is in charge of the class?

The ruler!

What member of the royal family
can you find in your school?

The *prince*-ipal!

Should you always do your homework with a smile?

No, it's better to use a pen or a pencil
to do your homework!

What furniture can you always
find in your school?

The multiplication *table*!

What is a mosquito's favorite subject in school?

Ar-*itch*-metic!

Why is 6 afraid of 7?

Because seven *ate* nine!

When you're having trouble with math,
what can you always count on for help?

Your fingers!

If you had two oranges and you ate one,
how many oranges would you have?

Two! One on the outside and one on the inside.

If you have six friends and only three apples, what's the best way to feed everyone?

Make applesauce!

How many feet are in a yard?

Twice as many as the number of
people standing in it!

Why did the silly goose feel sorry for the math book?

It had so many problems!

Why do witches always do so well at school?

They are good at *spell*-ing!

What bug gets the best grades in school?

The spelling bee!

Which letter comes after A in the alphabet?

All the letters come after A in the alphabet!

Did the silly goose like the joke about the dull pencil?

No. He thought it didn't have a point!

Why did all the kids want to play soccer during gym class?

They got a real kick out of it!

Which type of candy do teachers love best?

Chalk-olate!

What is the friendliest type of school?

Hi School!

Why did the hungry third grader run into the second-grade classroom?

He heard they were having a sub!

Why did the chicken cross the
playground?

To get to the other *slide*!

What is the longest word in the
school dictionary?

Smiles. There are *miles* after the first letter!

Where will you see the strangest
school play ever?

In the *odd*-itorium!

How did the silly goose get to the school nurse's office so fast?

Flu!

Why did the silly goose bring a Band-Aid to school?

He heard he was going on a class *trip*!

Why did the toothbrush wander into band practice?

It was looking for a *tuba* toothpaste!

When is a library book like a
watermelon?

When it is *red* inside!